I WISHED for YOU

✤ A KEEPSAKE ADOPTION JOURNAL ✤

Carrie Kipp Howard

sourcebooks

Published by Sourcebooks, Inc.
P.O. Box 4410, Naperville, Illinois 60567-4410
(630) 961-3900
Fax: (630) 961-2168
sourcebooks.com

Printed and bound in China.
LEO 10 9 8 7 6 5 4 3 2 1

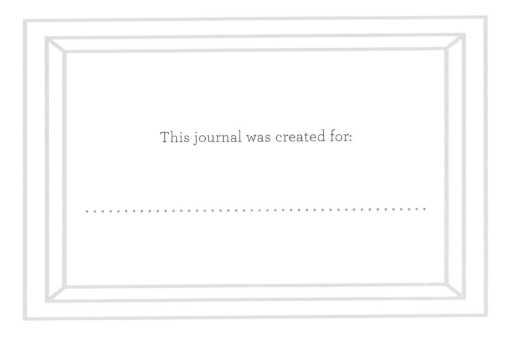

This journal was created for:

. . . .

FOREWORD

Waiting to bring home your child by adoption is a hopeful, stressful, exciting, and nerve-racking time. I know, because I've been there. My husband and I adopted three wonderful children—two as babies and one as an older child—and I spent many months thinking about my children-to-be, preparing for their arrival, and worrying about whether everything would work out all right. I dreamed about them at night and daydreamed about them during the day. Even though my children were far away, they were always in my heart and mind.

If you have started the adoption process and find that you are equally obsessed, relax—it's perfectly normal! Thinking and fretting about your future child is part of the process of becoming a parent. As an adoptive parent, you may not have a growing belly or a sonogram to point to as evidence that you

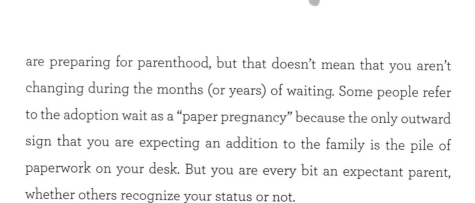

are preparing for parenthood, but that doesn't mean that you aren't changing during the months (or years) of waiting. Some people refer to the adoption wait as a "paper pregnancy" because the only outward sign that you are expecting an addition to the family is the pile of paperwork on your desk. But you are every bit an expectant parent, whether others recognize your status or not.

I Wished for You: A Keepsake Adoption Journal can serve two purposes during this exciting time. First, it is intended to give you an outlet for your feelings throughout the wait. Journaling can be a very healing process, giving you a chance to sort out your thoughts and get your fears off your chest and your hopes onto the page. The journal provides questions and prompts so that you can record your feelings throughout the adoption journey, and there are special pages where you can put photographs, mementos, or your own doodles or sketches. Second, the completed journal will become a keepsake that you can one day give to your child so that he or she will know how much you wished for them and loved them—even before you knew who they were.

This journal is designed to be used by all kinds of families. If a question or prompt doesn't apply to you or your family, just leave it blank. You can fill out the pages in any order that makes sense to you. The adoption process can be unpredictable, so jump around as much as you need to. No matter what your situation—whether you are hoping to bring home an infant, an older child, or a sibling group; adopting domestically, from foster care, through kinship, or internationally; adopting as a single parent or with a partner—you can use this journal however it best suits you and the child who will soon be part of your family. Take a deep breath, and enjoy the journey!

Taking the

FIRST STEPS

Here is a picture of me.

THE BIG DECISION

I have decided to adopt a child because ....

....

....

....

....

....

....

....

....

....

....

....

....

....

....

....

Since deciding to adopt, I have been feeling

(check all that apply):

☐ Overwhelmed. This is a complicated process!

☐ Peaceful. This feels exactly right.

☐ Curious. I wonder what adoption and parenting will be like?

☐ Excited! I can't wait to get going!

☐ ....

....

I have been thinking about adopting ever since ....

....

....

....

....

....

....

....

....

....

I plan to adopt *(circle one)* as a single parent / with my partner.
I am/we are feeling ....

....

....

....

This journal is mostly about my thoughts while waiting for you.
As I start this journey, I want you to know ....

....

....

....

....

....

Here is a picture of our family!

FAMILY AND FRIENDS

Besides me, lots of wonderful people are waiting to meet you, including

_____

_____

_____

_____

_____

_____

_____

And don't forget our pet(s), _____

_____

_____

Our home is a nice _____ located in _____

So far, I have told _____ about my plans to adopt.

I can't wait to tell _____

_____

_____

There will be many special people in your life. I think you're particularly
going to like ....
because ....

....

....

....

....

....

....

....

My hero is .... because ....

....

....

....

....

....

....

....

....

THINKING ABOUT PARENTHOOD

I am *(circle one)* a first-time / experienced parent. I have wanted to be a parent since I was

My parenting role models are

I *(circle one)* always / sometimes / never thought I would adopt a child. My plans for parenthood have changed over the years because

I want to be the kind of parent who ....

....

....

....

....

....

....

....

....

....

....

....

....

....

....

....

....

....

....

....

To me, the most important thing about parenting is

LEARNING ABOUT ADOPTION

I have been researching adoption and parenthood by attending

....

....

....

and reading ....

....

....

....

Some people involved in adoption who inspire me are ....

....

....

....

From them, I have learned ....

....

....

....

....

My favorite book or movie about adoption is

....

....

because ....

....

....

....

....

....

....

One thing I want you to know about adoption is ....

....

....

....

....

....

....

....

....

DECISIONS, DECISIONS

I have decided to adopt *(circle one)* an infant / older child from

....

....

....

....

....

I considered ....

....,

but ultimately chose this route to adoption because ....

....

....

....

....

....

....

....

....

....

I hope to work with ....

....

to adopt my child. I chose them because ....

....

....

....

....

....

....

It will be a long journey, but one thing I truly believe is ....

....

....

....

....

In fact, my motto is ....

....

....

....

....

GETTING READY

THE PAPER CHASE

I have submitted my application for adoption! I feel ....
....
....
....
....
....

Now I am starting the paperwork part of the process. There is a lot of
paperwork! I have filled out .... pages of forms and talked
to .... people.

Doing all this paperwork makes me feel ....
....
....
....
....

My partner is ....
....
....
....
....

The most embarrassing information I had to provide is ....

....

....

....

....

....

As part of the application, I need to write about my life, parenting plans, philosophical and spiritual beliefs, and reasons for adopting. It's a difficult task but a good one because it has made me reflect on

....

....

....

....

....

....

I would describe myself as ....

....

....

....

....

....

....

....

I think other people would say that I am ....

....

....

....

....

....

....

....

....

HOME STUDY

I had a home-study visit with ....

.... ,

who came to make sure our home is safe for a child and to discuss our family's parenting plans and expectations.

> **I got ready for the home-study visit by (check all that apply):**
>
> ☐ Cleaning, then cleaning some more.
>
> ☐ Childproofing everything.
>
> ☐ Making the house look cozy.
>
> ☐ Baking treats for the social worker (and eating them myself).
>
> ☐ ....
>
> ....

But I was so nervous I forgot to ....

....

....

....

....

....

The social worker made me feel ....

....

....

....

....

....

....

....

This is the first of .... visits we will have with our social worker.

Overall, I think the home-study visit went ....

....

....

....

....

....

....

....

....

....

MORE TO LEARN

I didn't realize that becoming a parent would mean going back to school! I have taken classes and seminars about ....

....

....

....

....

.... to get ready for you.

I'm doing assigned and personal reading too. Some of the books and articles I have read lately about parenting and adoption are ....

....

....

....

....

I have also been getting great advice from ....

....

....

....

....

I am learning so much! The thing I was most surprised to find out is

....

....

....

....

....

....

....

....

The most useful thing I have learned is ....

....

....

....

....

....

....

....

....

I got the good news today—our family's home study was approved!
The next step is to ....

....

....

....

....

....

....

....

I celebrated by ....

....

....

with ....

....

....

The adoption professionals I am working with think I will meet you
by ....

....

....

....

....

....

Sometimes I look at the moon and wonder if you can see it too. When
I try to imagine where you are right now and what you are doing, I
picture you ....

....

....

....

....

....

....

....

....

....

....

....

SHARING THE GOOD NEWS

I couldn't keep quiet! I've shared the good news about my upcoming adoption with ....

....

....

Here's how I told them: ....

....

....

....

The best response was ....

....

....

....

It made me feel ....

....

....

....

The funniest response was ....

....

....

....

....

....

....

....

Something you should know about the friends and family who are waiting for you here is that ....

....

....

....

....

....

....

....

....

....

....

Here is a picture of some things
that are waiting for you.

GIFTS FOR YOU

I admit it. I've already bought something for you!

It's a ....

....

I bought it because ....

....

....

....

....

And you are already receiving gifts!

We received ....

....

....

....

....

from ....

....

....

....

These things will be sitting ....

....

....

....

....

....

....

....

....

...., waiting for your arrival.

Someday, I hope I can give you _____

_____

_____

_____

_____

_____

_____

_____

_____

_____

Here is a token of my wishes for you.

WISHES FOR YOU

I have so many wishes for you—but mostly I wish to hold you in my arms. You were in my thoughts the last time I *(check all that apply)*:

- ☐ Wished on a star.
- ☐ Tossed a coin in a fountain.
- ☐ Blew out the candles on my birthday cake.
- ☐ Pulled apart a wishbone.
- ☐ Opened a fortune cookie.
- ☐ ....

I confess that sometimes I am superstitious about ....

....

....

My spiritual beliefs are ....

....

....

When you are older, I'll tell you about the time ....

....

....

Waiting for a
MATCH

THE WAIT BEGINS

The paperwork is (mostly) finished, and the approvals are in hand. Now I am just waiting to find out who you are. It's hard to wait, but there's so much I need to do, including ....

....

....

....

....

....

....

....

Currently my mood is (check all that apply):

☐ Pretty calm. There's no use worrying about things that are out of my control.

☐ Serene. I trust that all will be well.

☐ Mildly stressed. There's so much to do!

☐ Really worried. I can't stop thinking about things that can go wrong!

☐ ....

....

Although I haven't met you, I think about you constantly. I daydream about

Sometimes when I can't sleep, I just lie in bed thinking about ....

....

....

....

....

....

....

....

....

....

....

....

....

....

....

....

....

....

....

....

HOPING

I am full of hopes for the future. Of course I'll love you whoever you are, but right now *(circle one)* I am kind of hoping for a boy / girl / I don't care which gender because ....

....

....

....

....

....

....

I hope I *(circle one)* do / do not find out your gender ahead of time.

I hope your age will be about .... when we meet because ....

....

....

....

....

....

....

I hope you have ....

....

....

....

and can ....

....

....

....

But most of all, I hope ....

....

....

....

....

....

....

....

KEEPING BUSY

I am still learning about adoption and parenting!

Currently I am ....

....

....

....

....

....

It's helpful to talk to other adoptive parents and their children. I've joined some support groups, including ....

....

....

....

....

They have helped me ....

....

....

....

I also try to stay busy with other things to keep my mind off the wait.

I still spend time doing my usual activities, such as ....

....

....

....

I've even picked up some new interests, like ....

....

....

....

I know my life will change after you arrive, so while I still can, I'm

doing a lot of ....

....

....

....

....

....

....

....

....

....

....

UPS AND DOWNS

There have been a few bumps in the road, such as when ....
....
....
....
....
....

My response was to ....
....
....
....
....
....

The last time I cried was when ....
....
....
....
....

When I have a problem, my first reaction is usually to (check all that apply):

☐ Wait and see what happens.

☐ Pray for help.

☐ Meditate on a solution.

☐ Talk to my *(circle one or more)* partner / parent / best friend.

☐ Jump into action.

☐ ....

....

When you face challenges in life, I will help you to ....

....

....

....

....

....

....

....

....

....

....

THE NAME GAME

I have been thinking a lot about names. Right now my favorite names
for you are ....
and ....
....

These names are special to me because ....
....
....
....
....
....

My partner's favorite names are ....
and ....
because ....
....
....
....
....
....

Right now, my nickname for you is ....
....
....
....
....

I have always felt ....
....
....

about my own name because ....
....
....
....
....

When I become your parent, I think I would like you to call me
....

or maybe ....
but never ....
....
....

STAYING POSITIVE

Even though I am sometimes busy and stressed, I want to remember the good things that happen. The best news I have received recently is ....

....

....

....

....

....

....

Someone did something kind for me by ....

....

....

....

....

....

....

I did something kind for someone by ....

....

....

....

....

....

The last time I laughed was when ....

....

....

....

....

I can't wait for you to become part of our family routines. Every week,

we ....

....

....

....

....

....

....

....

DREAMTIME

I had a dream about you! In the dream, you ....

....

....

....

....

....

....

....

I think this dream means ....

....

....

....

....

....

....

....

The dream left me feeling ....

....

....

....

....

....

....

....

Do you dream at night? I believe that dreams are really about ....

....

....

....

....

....

....

....

....

STILL WAITING

Sometimes this wait seems very long. I want so much to hold you in my arms! I hope I will meet you before ....

....

so we can ....

....

....

....

....

One thing that has surprised me about the adoption process is how

....

....

.... I am.

I also notice that other people are ....

....

....

....

....

....

....

But other things have gone pretty much as I expected, such as ....

....

....

....

....

....

This wait is *(check all that apply)*:

☐ Okay. There's still so much to do to get ready.

☐ Annoying. Why does it have to take so long?

☐ Aggravating. Even elephants only have to wait two years to meet their child!

☐ Unbearable. I want to meet you *now!*

☐ ....

....

When I feel discouraged, I remember ....

....

....

....

....

....

TO-DO LIST

There are so many things I can't wait to do with you. I want to teach you how to ....

....

....

....

....

I want to play ....

....

....

....

.... with you.

I want you to meet ....

...., and I want to take you to ....

....

....

....

....

I really hope you like ....

....

....

....

....

....

....

My partner is hoping you are interested in ....

....

....

....

....

....

But it's okay if you have your own interests. Even if you like ....

....

....

....

....

....

....

But not ....

....

....

....

....

....

ALWAYS ON MY MIND

When I picture you, I imagine you looking

and doing

My partner thinks you are going to be

But you can be whatever you want. When I was a kid,
I wanted to grow up to be ....

....

....

....

....

....

....

The wait is especially hard around the holidays. My favorite holiday
is .... ,
and I can't wait to share it with you.

As time passes, you are becoming more real to me. Sometimes I talk
to you in my imagination or say a prayer for you. I usually say: ....

....

....

....

....

....

....

....

Making a

MATCH

THE BIG NEWS

Now I know who you are! Here's how I found out: ....
....
....
....
....
....
....
....
....
....
....
....
....
....
....
....
....
....
....

This is what I know about you now: ....
....
....
....
....
....
....
....
....

You will be waiting for us in ....
....
....
....
....
....
....
....

I was surprised that ....
....
....
....
....
....
....
....
....,

but not surprised that ....
....
....
....
....
....
....
....

I am feeling

My partner is

I celebrated by

with

The next step in the process is to ....

....

....

....

....

....

....

....

Now that I have some answers, I also have new questions! I'm dying

to know ....

....

....

....

....

....

....

....

....

Here is the first picture of you
that I saw.

FIRST LOOK

My heart is pounding. Now I know what you look like! I received a
picture of you that was taken ....

....

....

....

You looked .... and you were wearing ....

....

....

in the picture. You were about .... in age.

The first thing I noticed about you was your ....

....

....

....

....

....

....

....

When I saw your face, I felt *(check all that apply)*:

☐ A jolt of recognition, as if I already knew you.

☐ A vague sense of familiarity.

☐ Mild surprise. So that's who you are!

☐ Complete shock. You are not what I expected.
And that's okay!

☐ ....
....

I already think you are beautiful. I hope you always see yourself as

....

....

....

....

....

....

....

....

....

....

....

....

....

Here is our adoption announcement.

SPREADING THE NEWS

I let family and friends know about our match by ....
....
....
....
....
....
....
....
....

Their response was ....
....
....
....
....
....
....
....
....

I will always remember what ....

said: ....

The sweetest thing anyone has said about our adoption is ....

....

....

....

....

....

....

....

The weirdest thing anyone has said is ....

....

....

....

....

....

....

....

After you come home, I will send out an adoption announcement or let people know by ....

....

....

....

....

....

....

....

....

....

I know people will be excited as we announce by ....

....

....

....

....

....

....

....

....

....

....

GETTING TO KNOW YOU

I am learning more about you. Your birthday is / will be ....

....

I know this about your prenatal care and birth: ....

....

....

....

....

....

....

....

....

....

....

....

....

....

....

....

I also know that ....

....

....

....

....

....

....

I will travel to meet you around ....

....

....

....

I am feeling *(check all that apply)*:

☐ Over the moon! Things are getting real!

☐ Really excited! We are so close now!

☐ So nervous. Am I ready for this? Are you?

☐ Impatient. When can we get going?

☐ ....

....

I feel sad sometimes that I didn't know you when you were ....

....

....

....

....

....

....

But we will still have lots of time to ....

....

....

....

....

....

....

Now that I know who you are, I wish ....

....

....

....

....

....

....

....

....

....

....

....

....

Here is a map of where you're from.

WHERE YOU COME FROM

Here is what I know about the area you come from: ....

....

....

....

....

....

....

....

In the years ahead, it will be important for you to participate in the culture into which you were born. I will help you by ....

....

....

....

....

....

....

....

I will make sure that you have a chance to get to know people from your birth culture through

The world is a pretty ....
.... place right now.

I will always remember that while I was waiting for you, the news was
all about ....

....

....

....

....

....

....

....

....

....

....

....

....

....

....

FAMILY TIES

Here is what we know about your birth family: ....

....

....

....

....

....

....

....

I think about your birth family often. I know that placing you for adoption must have been a very difficult decision for them. From time to time, I send a thought or prayer their way with the wish that

....

....

....

....

....

....

....

In the future, we probably *(circle one)* will / will not
be able to have contact with your birth family
because ....

....

....

....

....

....

But we will always ....

....

....

....

....

I hope that you can someday know this about your birth family: ....

....

....

....

....

....

Things I have bought for you.

FEATHERING THE NEST

Now that I know who you are, I can go shopping in earnest. I have bought ....

....

....

....

....

....

....

....

I am also stockpiling ....

....

....

....

....

....

....

To be honest, I might have bought too many ....

....

....

....

....

....

....

If I have time, I am planning to make you a special ....

....

....

....

....

....

....

....

I can't wait to dress you in

....

....

....

....

....

....

I believe the most important thing to keep in mind when raising a child of your gender is

....

....

....

....

....

....

Here is a picture of our party.

WARM WELCOMES

Our friends and family had a *(circle one)* party / shower / gathering to welcome you! It was at ....

....,

and the theme was ....

....

....

....

....

....

....

The guests included ....

....

....

....

....

....

....

....

We ate ....

....

....

and enjoyed ....

....

....

Everyone is excited to meet you! We received so many lovely gifts,

including ....

....

....

....

I treasure these gifts as tokens of our friends' and family's love. My philosophy about gratitude is ....

....

....

....

....

....

....

....

....

Here is a picture of
where you'll sleep.

ROOM FOR YOU

Your room is almost ready! You will sleep in a ....
....

covered in a ....
....
....

The colors in your room are .... and ....

There's a picture of ....

on the wall. I chose it because ....
....
....
....
....
....
....

Sometimes I sit by your bed and imagine tucking you in and singing you a lullaby. I think the first song I sing to you will be ....

....

....

....

....

....

....

....

....

....

....

....

....

....

....

....

Even though I don't know you, I already love you. Getting your room ready is one way I can start taking care of you. Ultimately, I believe that love is ....

....

....

....

....

....

....

....

....

....

....

ARE WE THERE YET?

We are getting close, but I'm impatient! To make the time go faster,
I have been ....

....

....

....

....

....

I'm also working on my ....

....

.... skills.

I know that when we meet, I'm going to want to pick you up and give
you a big hug, and the trip to get you may involve some walking. So
I'm getting in shape by ....

....

....

....

....

....

While waiting for you, I have been *(check all that apply)*:

☐ Eating healthier than ever so I can be my best for you.

☐ Trying to eat healthy, but I didn't want to miss out on the cake at our party!

☐ Stress eating. I feel like I'm eating for two!

☐ Forgetting to eat. This is all so exciting!

☐ ....

....

The most challenging thing about this wait is ....

....

....

....

....

....

....

....

....

....

....

....

....

Becoming a
FAMILY

Here is a picture of me packing.

The time is getting close! I'm packing now. And maybe doing a little more shopping. Here are some of the things I'll take along when I meet you: ....

....

....

....

....

....

....

....

**Now that I think about it, I might have packed
(check all that apply):**

☐ Not enough. Let me check my list again.

☐ Too much. How am I going to carry all these suitcases?

☐ Not enough of some things, too much of others.

☐ Just the right amount—and there's room to bring back souvenirs!

☐ ....

....

I am still worried about

but I feel hopeful that

One thing I'm not worried about is ....

....

....

....

....

....

....

....

....

In the end, I know the most important thing I am bringing with me is

....

....

....

....

....

....

....

....

....

....

....

....

Here is our travel notice.

IT'S GO TIME!

I just got the word that I can come to meet you now! Here's how I
found out: ....

....

....

....

....

....

....

....

We will meet on .... at ....
I can't wait!

My travel plans are ....

....

....

....

....

....

....

I have _____ pictures of you now. From the pictures,

I can tell _____

_____

_____

_____

_____

_____

_____

I'm in a tizzy. Thank goodness I remembered to _____

_____

_____

_____

_____

_____

_____

_____

_____

One thing I know for sure is

TRAVEL NOTES

I am on my way to you! It's a ....

.... trip.

I am traveling .... from home

via ....

....

Traveling with me is ....

....

....,

who will help by ....

....

....

....

....

....

....

....

....

....

....

Leaving to bring you home makes me feel

(check all that apply):

☐ Excited! It's a new adventure.

☐ Calm. I'm a seasoned traveler.

☐ Nervous. I don't like traveling because ....
....

☐ Queasy. But it will be worth it!

☐ ....
....

I *(circle one)* have / have not visited your town before. Now that I'm here, I think it is ....

....

....

....

....

Do you know that we are coming? I have been told that you ....

....

....

....

....

Here is a picture of you
the day we met.

MEETING YOU

We have finally met! My first thought when I saw you was ....

....

....

....

My second thought was ....

....

....

....

The first thing I did was ....

....

....

....

The first thing you did was ....

....

....

....

....

Then we all ....

....

....

....

....

....

....

I'll never forget that you looked ....

....

....

....

....

....

....

....

Now that I really know your gender, age, and size, I feel ....

....

....

....

....

It's official: your name will be ....

....

Your name is special because ....

....

....

....

....

Becoming a Family

We now know more about your birth family: ....

....

....

....

....

....

....

....

And this is what we know about the people who have been caring for

you: ....

....

....

....

....

....

....

....

I will always be grateful to them for bringing you into the world and keeping you safe. If I could speak to them right now, I would say ....

....

....

....

....

....

One thing I want you to remember about your birth family is ....

....

....

....

....

....

One thing I want you to remember about your caregivers is ....

....

....

....

....

....

Here is our first picture together.

BECOMING A PARENT

I am the one taking care of you now! The first outfit I dressed you in
was ....

....

....

....

....

The first thing I fed you was ....

....

....

....

....

The first gift I gave you was ....

....

....

....

....

The first song I sang to you was ....

....

....

....

My partner likes to ....

....

....

....

.... with you.

I still have more forms to fill out and documents to sign, but the end is in sight. Now that we are together, I feel like the whole adoption process has been *(check all that apply)*:

☐ One of the hardest things I've ever done.

☐ A great chance to prepare for parenting.

☐ All but forgotten now that I have you in my arms.

☐ Not so bad. How would you feel about a sibling?

☐ ....

....

You are safe in your seat, and we are on our way home. You are

holding ....

and looking ....

....

....

As we started moving, you were *(check all that apply):*

☐ Crying.

☐ Sleeping.

☐ Quiet and watchful.

☐ Laughing and having fun.

☐ ....

....

I know now that your favorite food is .... ,

your favorite thing to do is ....

....

.... ,

and you always want ....

....

....

I am so grateful to ....

....

.... ,

who helped make this possible. And I am especially grateful to ....

....

....

....

....

....

....

When you are older, I hope you will have a chance to talk to ....

....

....

....

....

....

....

....

....

HOME AT LAST

Now we are home! Here's who was present to welcome you: ....

....

....

....

....

....

Your reaction when you entered our home was ....

....

....

....

....

The first thing you did was ....

....

....

....

....

When you saw your room, you ....

....

....

....

When you saw ....,

you ....

....

....

....

I hope you will always feel that home is a place where ....

....

....

....

My dearest wish has come true, because you are here with me. One part of our journey has ended, and another is just beginning. When you read this, I want you to know that, above all, ...

....

....

....

....

....

....

....

....

....

....

....

....

ABOUT THE AUTHOR

Carrie Kipp Howard is an award-winning writer and editor whose work has appeared in numerous books and publications. She has interests in branding and corporate identity, aviation, and parenting and adoption. A graduate of Pacific Lutheran University, she lives with her family in Seattle.

Photo credit: Maisie Howard

To Tessa, Maisie, and Lily, my wishes come true.

And to Andy, for wishing with me.